AF251061

PRESENTS:

FAST FOOD HACKS

TO SAVE MONEY & MORE!

Published by Mango Publishing, a division of Mango Publishing Group.
Cover Design: Unleash Media, Jade Catunao, Caroline Lackey
Layout Design: Unleash Media, Jade Catunao, Sebastian Günther
Cover Illustration: Unleash Media, Caroline Lackey, Danielle Caroli
Illustrations: Unleash Media, Jade Catunao, Caroline Lackey, Danielle Caroli

As a result of modifying the names of the brands within the book, the content needed to include some of the trade dress in order for readers to identify the products being discussed

For permission requests, please contact the publisher at:
Mango Publishing Group
2850 S Douglas Road, 2nd Floor
Coral Gables, FL 33134 USA
info@mango.bz

For special orders, quantity sales, course adoptions and corporate sales, please email the publisher at sales@mango.bz. For trade and wholesale sales, please contact Ingram Publisher Services at customer.service@ingramcontent.com or +1.800.509.4887.

HellthyJunkFood Presents: Fast Food Hacks to Save Money and More
Library of Congress Cataloging-in-Publication number: has been requested
ISBN: (pb) 978-1-68481-454-1 (e) 978-1-68481-455-8
BISAC: SOC022000, SOCIAL SCIENCE / Popular Culture

We are Julia and JP and we're here to walk you through the quirky, delicious, and sometimes really competitive world of fast food in the US.

And, best of all,
save you some money as you're enjoying your favorites.

Julia Goolia, also known as Julia Yarinsky, grew up in Saratoga Springs, surrounded by her six brothers. Growing up in a big family meant that Julia was often cooking and helping in the kitchen, developing her culinary skills and passion for food from a young age with guidance from her mother. She also started working in fine dining restaurants at a young age, gaining valuable experience in the food industry. After college, Julia struggled to find a job in her field of study, but her passion for food and entertainment led her to take a job at a restaurant, as a ticket puller at local shows, and as an account executive at a radio company developing marketing campaigns. During this time Julia got a gig as a cohost of a public access television show and as a host of an open mic, where she met JP.

Julia and JP hit it off immediately, and when Julia invited JP to come on her public access television show, they discovered they had great chemistry on camera. This led to JP inviting Julia to film a video with him where he ordered a hundred hash browns from McDonald's, and the two realized their shared passion for filming and creating junk food videos together. Their videos have since evolved from healthy to giant to food challenges and hacks, and they have gained a large following on social media. Despite her success, Julia remains hungry for more opportunities to create and share her love of food and entertainment with the world.

Julia Goolia

(aka Julia Yarinsky)

JP Lambiase is a South Korean adoptee who was raised by Italian parents. He arrived in the US with just one sock on, but he had a passion for food and comedy that would eventually lead him to YouTube stardom. JP's love for food began when he worked at Bill Greys in Rochester, where he learned valuable lessons about cooking. Meanwhile, he was always the class clown, and he worked tirelessly to hone his comedic skills. JP's comedic ambitions ultimately led him to meet Julia Goolia at the Oneonta Theatre.

They shared a love for junk food and started creating videos for fun. Initially, they aimed to make healthy junk food at home, but when they created a YouTube channel, they couldn't use that name. So, they decided to go with HellthyJunkFood, a playful name that allows them to explore all sorts of food-related concepts. Today, JP's goal is to share money-saving fast food hacks, tips, and tricks with a growing audience. His videos are entertaining, informative, and often hilarious. JP's unique background, combined with his passion for food and comedy, has made him a rising star in the world of YouTube.

JP Lambiase

Julia Goolia and JP Lambiase have collaborated to create this fast-food-hack-packed book. Stuffed with tips and tricks for your favorite fast-food chains, this book offers the best value for your money and fun ways to enjoy all the fast-food world has to offer.

Now that you know who we are and why we're so passionate about this, let's get started

Why do we have fast food?

Fa

Hist

And, more importantly,

Why do we love it so much?

st

Food

ory

Whether it's grabbing a quick dinner on the way home from a long day at work or a tasty snack after a night out with friends, fast-food options are endless and the perfect way to treat yourself when you most need it.

But where did this concept come from? Why are there so many options? And why is it such a staple of Americana culture? Those are just a few of the questions we hope to answer with this book as we dive into the stories of some of America's most iconic establishments and how to make their menu work for you and your wallet.

Fast food in the United States originated in the early 20th century as a response to a growing population and increased demand for quick, affordable meals. As these franchises evolved and imprinted on the consciousness of the 20th century, a few aspects took the lead as to what Americans wanted from their fast-food favorites:

Convenience, affordability, a wide variety of menu options, speed of service, social aspects, branding, and consistent quality.

Let's break these down to get a good understanding of how the hacks will improve your experience with each of them:

Convenience

Fast-food restaurants are known for their quick service and accessibility. They are often located in easily accessible areas, offer drive-thru options, and have extended operating hours. This makes them a convenient choice for busy individuals or families looking for a quick meal on the go.

Affordability

These venues generally offer inexpensive meal options, making them more affordable for many people. Value menus and combo meals provide a cost-effective way to satisfy hunger without breaking the bank. This affordability factor is particularly appealing for individuals or families on a tight budget.

Variety

They typically offer a wide range of menu options, catering to different tastes and preferences. They provide choices for breakfast, lunch, and dinner and often incorporate diverse cuisines and flavors into their offerings.

Social Aspects

Early on in fast-food history, the fast-food joints that had the most success could charge a little more because they were a gathering place for friends, families, and coworkers to hang out, eat for an inexpensive price and feel at home. Today, many of these restaurants offer a casual and relaxed environment where people can meet, socialize, and enjoy a meal together. This social aspect adds to the appeal of fast-food restaurants, particularly for those seeking a convenient and informal meeting spot.

Familiarity & Branding

Similar to the quality consistency is the feel consistency. The best fast-food chains established strong brand recognition and familiarity with consumers. Many people grew up with these brands and have developed a sense of loyalty or nostalgia towards them. The familiarity of the menu and the overall dining experience can create a sense of comfort and reassurance.

Consistent Quality

One of the biggest draws is the consistency in their food preparation and quality standards. Customers know what to expect when they visit these establishments, and this reliability can be comforting to many individuals. Additionally, standardized processes and training ensure that the taste and quality of the food remain consistent across different locations.

Speed of Service

Fast-food restaurants are designed to provide quick service. Orders are prepared and served rapidly, allowing customers to receive their meals in a short amount of time. This is especially attractive for individuals who are in a hurry or have limited time for lunch breaks.

While it's important to note that excessive consumption of fast food can have negative health effects, the benefits mentioned on the last few pages help explain why fast-food restaurants remain popular in the United States.

In this book we'll cover some of America's most popular establishments as we celebrate their history, menus, and more. Let's get to know them a little better so that when you begin saving money, you'll have a great understanding of what got us here.

The Big Players

McDonald's, founded in 1940 by Richard and Maurice McDonald, is widely recognized as one of the pioneers of the fast-food industry. They introduced the Speedee Service System, which emphasized speedy preparation and assembly line-style production. McDonald's became a symbol of the fast food culture and eventually expanded globally.

In-N-Out grew out of the early momentum, looking to really play up the experience aspect of 1940s burgers.

Burger King, established in 1954, adopted a similar model to McDonald's, offering flame-broiled hamburgers and drive-thru service. The Whopper, introduced in 1957, became their signature sandwich.

Wendy's followed, founded by Dave Thomas in 1969, and distinguished itself by offering square-shaped hamburgers and a salad bar. They focused on using fresh ingredients and made-to-order meals.

Taco Bell, coming a few years before Wendy's, brought Mexican-inspired fast food to the mainstream. Their menu featured items like tacos, burritos, and nachos, catering to a growing demand for ethnic flavors.

Subway introduced the concept of customizable submarine sandwiches. They emphasized freshly baked bread and a variety of toppings.

Established in 1971, Starbucks was originally focused on coffee beans and beverages. It gradually expanded its menu to include pastries, sandwiches, and snacks, transforming into a popular coffeehouse chain.

Popeyes, like Subway and Taco Bell, aimed to set itself apart. It specialized in Louisiana-style fried chicken and seafood dishes. They gained popularity for their spicy chicken offerings.

By the late eighties, the original kings of fast food were starting to see consumers question one of the key values established early on: consistent quality. That's when Five Guys, founded in 1986, gained recognition for its high-quality burgers and fries. They emphasized simple menu options, fresh ingredients, and a no-frills dining experience.

Chipotle popped up in 1993 and blended some of what Taco Bell and Subway did so well decades ago: a fast-casual dining experience, offering burritos, tacos, and bowls with a focus on customizable and fresh ingredients. Chipotle emphasized using sustainably sourced and naturally raised ingredients.

Now that we've got all that covered, let's jump in, save some money, and enjoy some delicious comforts foods.

The Ultimate Table of Contents

#001 FOR HELLTHY...
FAST FOOD HACKS

HACK COUNT: 106
TOTAL SAVINGS: A:LOT

THANK YOU FOR VISITING!

31012 21532826 1866435 45880

CARD #: **** **** **** 2023
THANKS: 140

WHERE'S MY HACK

#002 FOR JP
FAST FOOD HACKS

HACK COUNT: 106
TOTAL SAVINGS: A:LOT

HOPE TO SEE YOU AGAIN!

45898 10244653 85687263 14023

TABLE OF CONTENTS

#001 FOR HELLTHYJUNKFOOD
FAST FOOD HACKS

HACK COUNT:
TOTAL SAVIN...

THAN...

CARD #...
THANK...

WHERE'S MY HACK?

#003 FOR JULIA
FAST FOOD HACKS

HACK COUNT: 106
TOTAL SAVINGS: A:LOT

THANK YOU FOR VISITING!

32039 DESIGNED BY UNLEASH MEDIA 0489

WHAT PAGE DO I GO TO?

#001 FOR HELLTHYJUNKFOOD
FAST FOOD HACKS

WHERE'S MY HACK?

#001 FOR HELLTHYJUNKFOOD
FAST FOOD HACKS

BORGER
KONG

Fancy Bun

Effort Level: 1/5

Savings: 1/5

Hack Level: 1/5

1. Order whatever you want.
2. Say *"Can I get that on a brioche bun?"*
3. Get that beautifully rich and buttery artisanal roll for absolutely no extra charge.

The Martin's Potato Rolls 24 pack are $3.99.

The Borger Kong 20 piece nugget is $2.98.

(plus there's 6 free sauces)

37¢ Sliders

Effort Level: ●●●●○

Savings: ●●●●●

Hack Level: ●●●●○

---

1. Buy a pack of 2 dozen rolls.
2. Buy a 20 piece nugget and get *alllllllll* the sauces.
3. Take a roll, break it open, dip your nugget in your sauce, stuff it in a roll, and take a bite.

Between the Whopper Junior and our Budget Whopper:

✖ The Whopper Junior weighs less. ✔

•_• The patties are the exact same size. •‿•

✖ The Whopper Junior doesn't even have bacon. ✔

Budget Whopper

Effort Level: ▮▮▮▯▯

Savings: ▮▮▯▯▯

Hack Level: ▮▯▯▯▯

---

1. On the mobile app, order a bacon cheeseburger for $1.
2. Add mayo, remove mustard, choose light lettuce (regular costs money!) and add extra tomato.
3. Enjoy your fresh Budget Whopper!

**onions and pickles are free WOO HOO!*

Better Sandwich

(That's right. Fries on the sammy.)

Free Fries
Free Fries

Free Fries

Effort Level: ●●●●○

Savings: ●●●●●

Hack Level: ●●●●○

---

1. Order whatever sandwich you want.
2. Say *"Can I get a massive amount of fries on top?"* *(*you can also ask for onion rings!!)*
3. Get fries on top of your sandwich at no extra charge.

VARIETY IS THE SPICE OF LIFE

Two For One

Effort Level: 2/5

Savings: 1/5

Hack Level: 3/5

1. Order a medium fry...or small or large.
2. Say *"Can you make it half and half onion rings?"*
3. Get a side of zesty sauce and enjoy the best of both worlds.

Don't ever order small size hashbrowns, the medium is only 10 cents more and it's double the calories, meaning double the amount!

Don't Ever Get These

Effort Level: 1/5

Savings: 4/5

Hack Level: 3/5

1. Visit Borger Kong in the morning.
2. Order a medium size hashbrown for $1.69.
3. Enjoy double the breakfast for a price your wallet will be happy with. Don't get ripped off.

THE FRONT

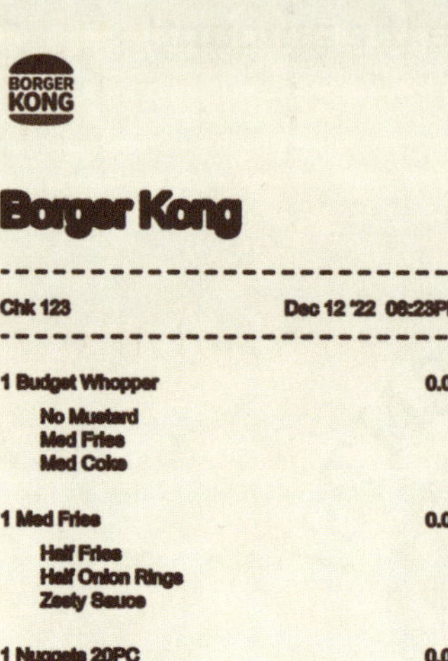

✦ THE BACK ✦

BK Receipt

Effort Level: 1/5

Savings: 3/5

Hack Level: 1/5

1. Do one of our other Borger Kong hacks.
2. Ask for the receipt.
3. It will always have some awesome coupon on the back. With a simple survey, *you* can get *NOT* ripped off.

FANCY
BUN

37 CENT
SLIDERS

BUDGET
WHOPPER

FREE
FRIES

TWO FOR
ONE

DON'T EVER
GET THESE

BK
RECEIPT

Chalk-Fil-A

Free Rewards

Effort Level: 1/5

Savings: 2/5

Hack Level: 2/5

1. Go to the Chalk-Fil-A app and go to Rewards.
2. Navigate to Upload > Upload by Receipt.
3. Upload your receipts, your friends' receipts, heck even receipts from the trash! All for free points!

Budget Combo

Effort Level: 1/5
Savings: 3/5
Hack Level: 4/5

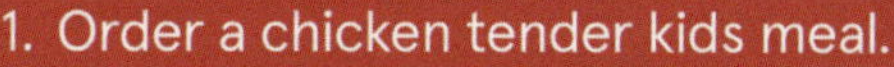

1. Order a chicken tender kids meal.
2. Ask for a bun, a side of pickles, fries, a lemonade with no ice, and an ice cream instead of a toy.
3. Enjoy!

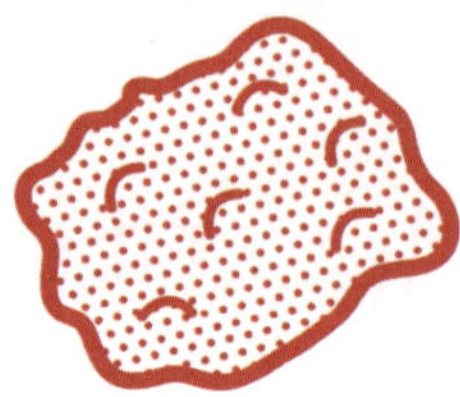

Buffalo Mac N' Cheese

Effort Level: 1/5

Savings: 1/5

Hack Level: 4/5

1. Order a kid's 5pc chicken nugget meal, get mac n' cheese as your side, and buffalo and ranch sauces.
2. Pour ya buffalo sauce on nuggets, shake to mix, then dump it on top of the mac and cheese.
3. Drizzle on ranch dressing and enjoy!

— THIS IS A PSA —

Your average sandwich is pre-made

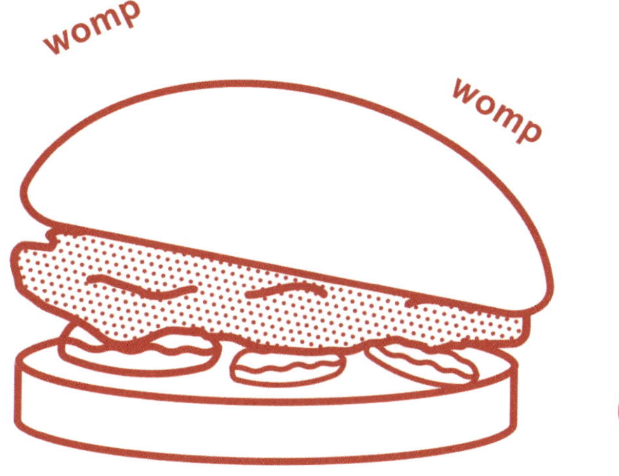

(making it not as fresh when you receive it)!

No Soggy

Effort Level: ●○○○○

Savings: ○○○○○

Hack Level: ●●●○○

1. Visit your local Chalk-fil-A during their open hours.
2. Order a Chalk-fil-A sandwich with pickles on the side (instead of on the sandwich).
3. Enjoy your fresh sandwich and even more pickles!

5LBS

OF THE BEST ICE

It's a special shape that doesn't melt as fast, keeping your drink cold without diluting it...and it's only $1.59!

Sonic Ice

Effort Level: 1/5

Savings: 2/5

Hack Level: 5/5

1. Visit Chalk-fil-A at any time of day.
2. Ask for a bag of ice (it's freshly scooped)!
3. Enjoy your fresh bag of perfectly chewable ice at a great price.

Free Sandwich

Effort Level: 1/5

Savings: 4/5

Hack Level: 5/5

1. Download the Chalk-fil-A app to your phone.
2. Create an account.
3. Receive your sign on reward for a free sandwich. Use this hack infinitely with different emails!

Side Salad Wrap

Effort Level: ●○○○○
Savings: ●●○○○
Hack Level: ●●●○○

1. Order a side salad + any additional toppings you'd like. Also order a wrap by itself.
2. Pull out your Chipottel skills and create your wrap.
3. Voila! You have yourself a wrap for half the price!

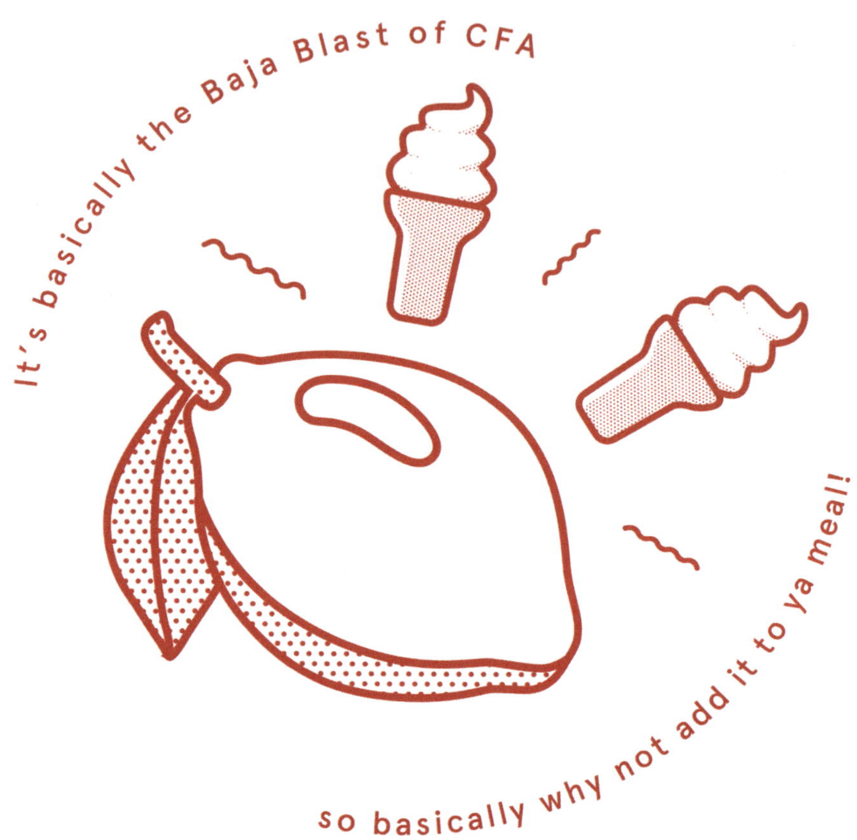

Frosted Lemonade

Effort Level: 1/5
Savings: 4/5
Hack Level: 4/5

1. When ordering a kids meal, get an ice cream instead of the toy and a lemonade with no ice.
2. Put your ice cream into your lemonade and stir.
3. Enjoy saving $3.75 on a frosted lemonade!

FREE
REWARDS

BUDGET
COMBO

BUFFALO MAC
'N CHEESE

NO
SOGGY

SONIC
ICE

FREE
SANDWICH

SIDE SALAD
WRAP

FROSTED
LEMONADE

CHIPOTTEL

THREE DOLLAR BURRITO

Effort Level: ●○○○○

Savings: ●●●●●

Hack Level: ●●●●○

1. Go to the app and order one taco with any meat.
2. Add rice, beans, and any toppings (on the side).
3. Add a tortilla (on the side as well) and assemble your burrito.

KIDS MEAL MEAT HACK

Effort Level: ●○○○○

Savings: ●●●○○

Hack Level: ●●●○○

---

1. Order a kids meal at Chipottel.
2. Select any meat of your choosing, considering that all meat is the same price as chicken!
3. Enjoy your wallet-friendly meal.

SOFT TACO

WITH STEAK &

Cheese

& A SIDE OF ....

SOUR CREAM

& VINAIGRETTE

STEAK QUESADILLA

Effort Level: ●●○○○

Savings: ●○○○○

Hack Level: ●●●●○

1. Order a taco at Chipottel.
2. Add steak, fajitas, and cheese with a side of sour cream and vinaigrette.
3. When you get home, grill it on both sides and enjoy a quesadilla for only $4.48.

LOADED NACHOS

Effort Level: ●●○○○

Savings: ●●●●●

Hack Level: ●●○○○

1. Order a kids meal (because any meat is $4.95).
2. Ask for hard shells, beans, rice, and every topping on the side.
3. Crumble up the chips and hard shells, and pour them all on top with toppings!

FREE BURRITO

Effort Level: ●○○○○

Savings: ●○○○○

Hack Level: ●●●●○

1. Order a bowl at Chipottel.
2. Get both rices, both beans, half and half meats, and every topping with two tortillas on the side.
3. Scoop half of the bowl into each tortilla and enjoy two for the price of one!

MOBILE ORDERS TAKE LONGER & HAVE LESS FOOD

DON'T ORDER ONLINE

Effort Level: ●○○○○

Savings: ●○○○○

Hack Level: ●●●●●

1. Go to your local Chipottel.
2. Hop in line and order your desired meal.
3. Enjoy waiting a shorter time and getting more food compared to ordering online.

THREE DOLLAR BURRITO

KIDS MEAL MEAT HACK

STEAK QUESADILLA

LOADED NACHOS

FREE BURRITO

DON'T ORDER ONLINE

1 SCOOPIE TOKEN

The butter burger in the kid's meal is the SAME SIZE as the regular, adult butter burger.

FOR 10 CENTS:
Get a larger fry or sub fruit or veggies

SCOOPIE TOKENS = 1 FREE MEAL

KID'S MEAL PERKS

EFFORT LEVEL: ●●○○○

SAVINGS: ●●●○○

HACK LEVEL: ●●●●●

1. Order a kid's meal.
2. Try any of the hacks shown to the left, even try multiple in the same order.
3. Have yourself a very cost-effective meal!

SCOOPIE TOKEN

There's more drink options in a kid's meal...you can even sub it with ice cream!

SHRIMP PO BOY HACK

EFFORT LEVEL: ●●○○○

SAVINGS: ●○○○○

HACK LEVEL: ●●●●○

1. Order 6 jumbo shrimps.
2. Order the following sides: a hoagie bun, lettuce, tomatoes, pickles, and anything else you'd like.
3. Assemble your shrimp po boy with all the ingredients!

POUTINE HACK

EFFORT LEVEL: 1/5

SAVINGS: 1/5

HACK LEVEL: 4/5

1. Order a large fry, a large side of cheese curds, and two sides of beef gravy.
2. Toss your ingredients together.
3. Enjoy some good ol' poutine!

BUDGET BURGER

EFFORT LEVEL: 1/5

SAVINGS: 3/5

HACK LEVEL: 4/5

---

1. Order yourself a kid's meal.
2. The butter burger in the kid's meal is the same size as the adult version.
3. Keep your wallet and stomach full with this hack!

10 CENT UPGRADE

EFFORT LEVEL: ●○○○○

SAVINGS: ●●●○○

HACK LEVEL: ●●●○○

1. Order a kid's meal.
2. Ask to upgrade your small fry to a medium fry.
3. They'll make this change for only 10 cents more AND you'll get so many more fries!

FREE MILKSHAKE

EFFORT LEVEL: ●○○○○

SAVINGS: ●●●●○

HACK LEVEL: ●●●●○

---

1. Order a kid's meal.
2. Get a milk for your drink and any flavor custard that you'd like to indulge in.
3. Mix the two together and you've got a milkshake!

FREE ICE CREAM

EFFORT LEVEL: ●○○○○

SAVINGS: ●●●●●

HACK LEVEL: ●●○○○

1. Before you order, go to tellculvers.com and click on the 'Start' button three times.
2. Click 'Next' until you reach the end of the survey.
3. Use the code when you order to get FREE ice cream!

BIG MAC HACK

EFFORT LEVEL: 2/5

SAVINGS: 0/5

HACK LEVEL: 3/5

1. Order a butter burger with cheese.
2. Add double meat, extra pickles, extra lettuce, a side of thousand island dressing, and a bun on the side.
3. Combine everything together for your big mac!

SECRET SUBSTITUTE

EFFORT LEVEL: ▮▯▯▯▯

SAVINGS: ▯▯▯▯▯

HACK LEVEL: ▮▮▮▯▯

1. Order a concrete mixer with these toppings: cherry, butter cake, and dove chips.
2. This used to be a limited time item during Christmas.
3. Now have a secret, special item to enjoy year-round.

KIDS MEAL PERKS

SHRIMP PO BOY HACK

POUTINE HACK

BUDGET BURGER

10 CENT UPGRADE

FREE MILKSHAKE

FREE ICE CREAM

BIG MAC HACK

SECRET SUBSTITUTE

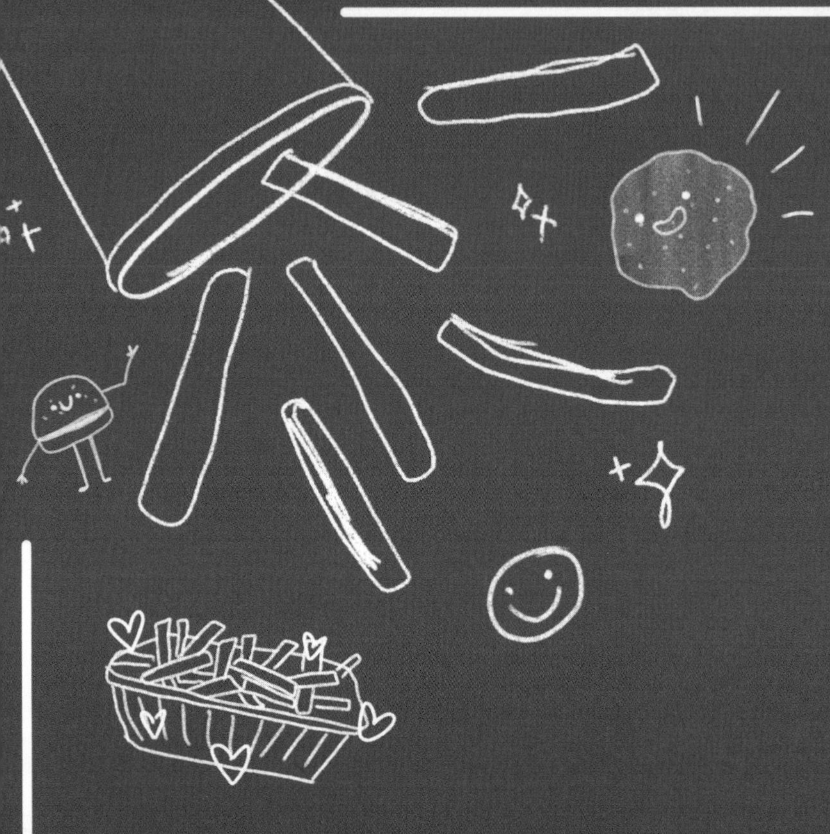

FRIED GUYS

BRAGERS and FREES

BEST SIZE FRIES

EFFORT LEVEL: ●●○○○

SAVINGS: ●●●●○

HACK LEVEL: ●●●●○

1. If you're ordering more than one order of fries at Fried Guys, order them in separate bags.
2. Due to their scooping method, you'll get more fries this way.
3. The regular is only 90 cents more than the little. Enjoy more!

PATTY MELT

EFFORT LEVEL: ●○○○○

SAVINGS: ●●●●●

HACK LEVEL: ●●●●●

1. *Go to Fried Guys and ask for a grilled cheese.*
2. Ask for two additional patties and as many toppings as you would like.
3. Enjoy spending less than you would the normal way!

LOADED FRIES

EFFORT LEVEL: ●●●●○

SAVINGS: ●○○○○

HACK LEVEL: ●●○○○

1. Order a little bacon cheeseburger, no bun, chopped, any toppings on the side (they're free) and add a little fry.
2. Put your fries in a tin foil container and pour on the toppings.
3. Add a ketchup drizzle and enjoy the best way to eat Fried Guys.

FREE BURGER

EFFORT LEVEL: ●●○○○

SAVINGS: ●●●●●

HACK LEVEL: ●●●●○

1. *Go to Fried Guys and order a cheeseburger wlth all of the toppings on the side.*
2. *Be sure to ask for an extra bun (they're free).*
3. *Build both your burgers exactly the way you like them.*

- hot sauce
- mustard
- A1
- BBQ sauce
- mayo
- relish
- peppers
- jalapeños
- Mushrooms
- grilled onions
- pickles
- tomatoes
- lettuce
- napkins
- knife
- fork
- vinegar
- ketchup
- salt
- pepper
- straw
- whatever fries in the bag

ALL COMPLIMENTARY

FREE ITEMS

EFFORT LEVEL: ●●○○○

SAVINGS: ●●●●○

HACK LEVEL: ●●●●○

1. When ordering at Fried Guys, most of your toppings are complimentary!
2. While placing your order, ask for your desired toppings.
3. Enjoy!

BEST FRY SIZES

PATTY MELT

LOADED FRIES

FREE BURGER

FREE ITEMS

McDoodles

Best Way to Eat McDoodles

Effort Level: ●○○○○

Savings: ●○○○○

Hack Level: ●●●●○

---

1. Order a medium fry with no salt and a medium cup with salt packets.
2. Shake up the salt with the fries in the cup.
3. Enjoy your fresh cup fries AND burger holder.

Ice Cream Sandwich Hack

Effort Level: ●○○○○

Savings: ●○○○○

Hack Level: ●●●●●

1. Order 2 cookies and any sundae/McFlurry.
2. Assemble your ice cream sandwich *(a life skill you probably have)* and freeze it.
3. Now you can enjoy your sweet, delicious treat.

Drink Debunk

Effort Level: ●○○○○

Savings: ●●●○○

Hack Level: ●●●○○

1. Understand that there's barely a difference between the small, medium, and large sizes.

   Hack 1: Use the app coupon for $1 drinks.

   Hack 2: Always order a small for best value.

Chicken Big Mac

Effort Level: ●○○○○

Savings: ○○○○○

Hack Level: ●●●○○

1. Order a Big Mac but with chicken patties instead of the beef patties.
2. Receive your special request mac.
3. Enjoy!

Best Size Fries

Effort Level: ●○○○○

Savings: ●●●●○

Hack Level: ●●●○○

1. Go to the McDoodle's app and go to Deals.
2. You'll find a Large Fry for only $1, and it's valid every single day!
3. Coupon or not, the large is the best value fry.

Coffee Sundae

Effort Level: ●○○○○

Savings: ○○○○○

Hack Level: ●●●●●

1. Order yourself a hot coffee, a large cup, and a hot fudge sundae.
2. Pour the coffee and the sundae into the cup.
3. Mix it up and enjoy the deliciousness.

The Real McDoodles Milkshake

Effort Level: ●●○○○

Savings: ●●●●○

Hack Level: ●●●●○

1. Order a milk, regular or chocolate.
2. Order a vanilla cone.
3. Mix them in an extra cup and now you have a delicious milkshake with actual milk!

Best Ice Cream Size

Effort Level: ●○○○○

Savings: ●●●○○

Hack Level: ●●●○○

1. There's a small difference between the cone, sundae, and McFlurry amounts of ice cream.
2. To get the best value, always order the cone.
3. Use this hack to stop getting ripped off!

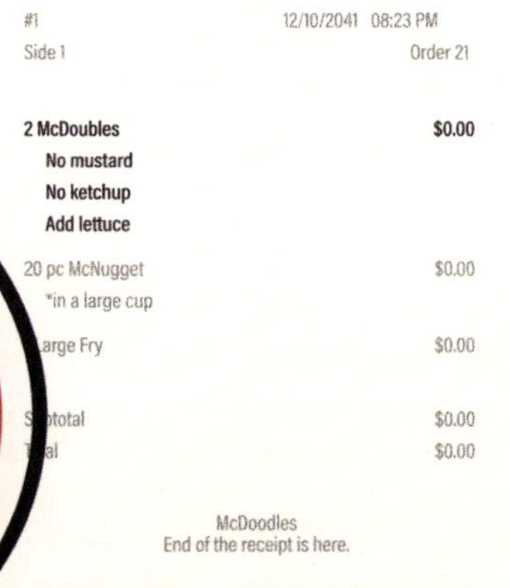

Ask for mac sauce on the side!
(after ordering)

Budget Big Mac

Effort Level: ●●○○○

Savings: ●●○○○

Hack Level: ●●○○○

---

1. Order 2 McDoubles with no mustard, no ketchup, and add lettuce.
2. After ordering, ask for a side of mac sauce.
3. Assemble your faux Big Mac with 2x the meat!

Orange Julius

Effort Level: ●○○○○

Savings: ●○○○○

Hack Level: ●●●○○

1. Get orange soda, Fanta will do.
2. Add creamer into your drink and mix it up.
3. Enjoy your orange creamsicle drink, aka an Orange Julius!

creamy Ranch

spicy Buffalo

Buffalo Chicken Fries

Effort Level: ●●○○○

Savings: ○○○○○

Hack Level: ●●●○○

---

1. Order a 4pc Chicken Nugget Happy Meal with Spicy Buffalo and Ranch sauces.
2. Ask for a Big Breakfast container.
3. Add everything from the meal, shake, & enjoy!

The McDonut Burger

Effort Level: ▮OOOO

Savings: ▮OOOO

Hack Level: ▮▮▮▮O

1. Get a bacon double quarter pounder with cheese, toppings, and 2 pull-apart donuts.
2. Put half of the quarter pounder on each donut.
3. Enjoy your sweet & savory sandwiches!

McRib Mac

Effort Level: ●●○○○

Savings: ○○○○○

Hack Level: ●●●●●

1. Order a Big Mac with no mac sauce, lettuce, or cheese, then add extra pickles and onions.
2. Get 2 bbq sauces and coat the patties in them.
3. Reassemble your burger and there you go!

Free Sauces

Effort Level: ●○○○○

Savings: ●●●●●

Hack Level: ●●●●●

1. Did you know that on the McDoodle's app, all the condiments *(besides syrup)* are free?
2. Order up to 20 sauces per mobile order!
3. Relish in your non-relish, sauce-y glory.

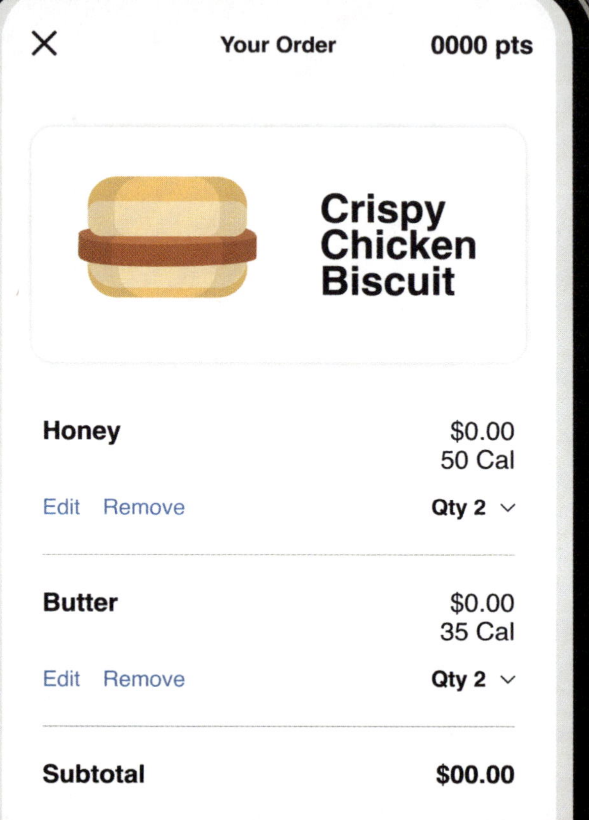

Honey Butter Biscuit

Effort Level: ●○○○○

Savings: ●●●●○

Hack Level: ●●○○○

1. At breakfast, order the crispy chicken biscuit and add 2 sides of honey and butter each.
2. Put the butter on the chicken. *(The heat makes it melt!)*
3. Drizzle on the honey and enjoy.

Quarter Pounder Big Mac

Effort Level: ●○○○○

Savings: ●○○○○

Hack Level: ●●●●●

---

1. Order a Double Quarter Pounder.
2. Ask them to make it like a Big Mac.
3. Enjoy your better than ever Big Mac with that quality meat rather than sad lil patties.

Budget McFlurry

Effort Level: ●●○○○

Savings: ●●●○○

Hack Level: ●●○○○

1. Order an ice cream cone and add whatever toppings you'd like, but on the side in a cup.
2. Dump your ice cream into the toppings cup.
3. Stir it together to get your budget McFlurry!

Free Upgrade

Effort Level: ●○○○○

Savings: ●○○○○

Hack Level: ●●●○○

1. Order your breakfast sandwich of choice.
2. Substitute the folded egg with a round egg or even the opposite way!
3. McDoodle's will do this for you for no extra cost!

Big Breakfast Sandwich

Effort Level: ●○○○○

Savings: ●●●●○

Hack Level: ●●○○○

1. Order yourself a Big Breakfast.
2. Construct yourself a sausage biscuit w/ egg.
3. Enjoy a sandwich, hashbrown, and pancakes for a great breakfast!

Best Way to Eat a Big Mac

Effort Level: ●○○○○

Savings: ○○○○○

Hack Level: ●●○○○

1. Order a Big Mac.
2. Toss the top bun. From the top patty to the middle bun, hold it & flip it so the bun is on top.
3. Consume without the unnecessary carbs!

Fries Hack

Effort Level: ●○○○○

Savings: ●●○○○

Hack Level: ●●●○○

1. Order a large fry.
2. Ask for your fries to be put into a large cup.
3. Enjoy the extra fries and your travel-friendly container.

Nuggets Cup

Effort Level: ●○○○○

Savings: ○○○○○

Hack Level: ●●●○○

1. Say *"Can I get a 20 piece McNugget, but can you put it in a large cup?"*
2. Receive 20 nuggets in a large cup.
3. Enjoy your car-friendly nuggets meal!

BEST WAY TO EAT MCDOODLES

ICE CREAM SANDWICH HACK

DRINK DEBUNK

CHICKEN BIG MAC

BEST SIZE FRIES

COFFEE SUNDAE

THE REAL MCDOODLES MILKSHAKE

BEST ICE CREAM SIZE

BUDGET BIG MAC

ORANGE JULIUS

BUFFALO CHICKEN FRIES

THE MCDONUT BURGER

MCRIB
MAC

FREE
SAUCES

HONEY BUTTER
BISCUIT

QUARTER
POUNDER BIG MAC

BUDGET
MCFLURRY

FREE
UPGRADE

BIG BREAKFAST
SANDWICH

BEST WAY TO EAT
A BIG MAC

FRIES
HACK

NUGGETS
CUP

Mendy's

CHILI CHEESE BURGER

EFFORT LEVEL: ●○○○○

SAVINGS: ●○○○○

HACK LEVEL: ●●●●●

1. Pursue your Wendy's order by whatever means you typically do — in store, drive thru, app, etc.
2. Say *"Can I get ______ burger with chili on it?"*
3. Enjoy!

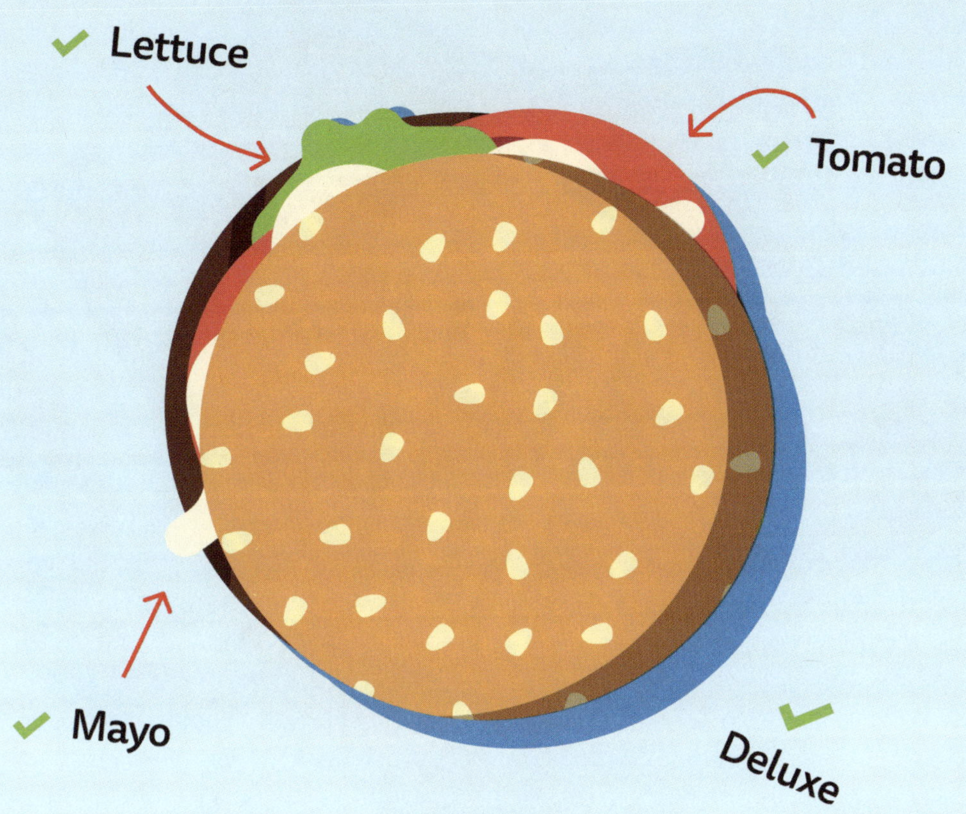

MAKE IT DELUXE

EFFORT LEVEL: ●○○○○

SAVINGS: ●●○○○

HACK LEVEL: ●●●○○

1. Go to the Wendy's app.
2. Order a Junior Cheeseburger and add lettuce, tomato, and mayonnaise for no extra charge!
3. Get a Deluxe burger without a deluxe price.

FREE FROSTY

EFFORT LEVEL: ●○○○○

SAVINGS: ●●●●●

HACK LEVEL: ●●●●●

1. Order a frosty key tag for $2.
2. Now you have a year of free junior frosties anytime you stop by Wendy's!
3. Plus you donated to charity.

BACON DOUBLESTACK

- ⊘ Mustard
- ⊘ Pickles
- ⊘ Onions
- ✓ Mayo
- ✓ Premium Bun

THE BUDGET BACONATOR

EFFORT LEVEL: ●●○○○

SAVINGS: ●●○○○

HACK LEVEL: ●●●○○

1. Say *"Can I get a bacon double stack with ketchup and mayo only, and on a premium bun?"*
2. Get a burger just like the Son of Baconator burger.
3. Save a lil over $2 with this hack!

THE BREAKFAST BACONATOR

EFFORT LEVEL: ●○○○○
SAVINGS: ●●○○○
HACK LEVEL: ●●●●●

1. Go to Wendy's right before breakfast ends.
2. Order a Breakfast Baconator with a hamburger patty instead of sausage.
3. Enjoy the even better Breakfast Baconator!

CHILI CHEESE BURGER

MAKE IT DELUXE

FREE FROSTY

THE BUDGET BACONATOR

THE BREAKFAST BACONATOR

NACHO
BELL

THE $2 QUESARITO

EFFORT LEVEL: ●●○○○

SAVINGS: ●●●○○

HACK LEVEL: ●●●○○

1. Order a beef burrito and a chicken chipotle melt.
2. Ask them to grill it (it's free).
3. Unfold your chicken chipotle melt, plop down your burrito, and roll them together to make your quesarito.

MEXIMELT HACK

EFFORT LEVEL: ●●○○○
SAVINGS: ●○○○○
HACK LEVEL: ●●●○○

1. Order a cheesy roll up with beef and tomatoes.
2. Receive the cheesy roll up.
3. Enjoy the cheesy, beefy goodness of this DIY meximelt moment.

NO MESS TACO

EFFORT LEVEL: ●●○○○

SAVINGS: ●●●○○

HACK LEVEL: ●●●●○

1. Order a crunchy taco, nacho cheese, and a flour tortilla.
2. Pour the cheese onto the tortilla, then put your taco on top of both and fold it together.
3. Now you have a safety tortilla to hold your toppings!

THE DESSERT BURRITO

EFFORT LEVEL: ●●○○○

SAVINGS: ●○○○○

HACK LEVEL: ●●●●●

1. Prepare your second stomach for dessert.
2. Order a large flour tortilla, 4 cinnabons, and get an order of cinnamon twists.
3. Assemble these items into burrito form and enjoy.

HACK THE SURVEY

1. Go to tellthebell.com & ignore all instructions. Click 'Start' 2x and click 'Next' 10x.
2. At the sweepstakes question, reply yes.
3. Enter your info and get your chance to win $500.

50 CENT NACHO FRIES

EFFORT LEVEL: 1/5
SAVINGS: 3/5
HACK LEVEL: 5/5

1. Get on the Nacho Bell app.
2. Go to Sides > Black Beans > Customize > Add Ons.
3. They'll have seasoned fries for only $0.50 and you can even put them separate so you don't get weird bean fries.

GET FREE FOOD

EFFORT LEVEL: ●○○○○

SAVINGS: ●●●○○

HACK LEVEL: ●●●●○

1. Downloads the Nacho Bell app.
2. Sign up for Nacho Bell rewards *(you can even use an old email address to do this multiple times).*
3. Get a free burrito or taco!

60 CENT RICE & POTATOES

EFFORT LEVEL: 1/5
SAVINGS: 3/5
HACK LEVEL: 4/5

1. Go to the Nacho Bell app and order any item.
2. You can add rice and/or potatoes for only $0.60 each.
3. Make sure to click "On the side" so that they give you a ginormous proportion, rather than whatever fits in your lil taco.

THE $1 QUESADILLA

EFFORT LEVEL: ●●○○○

SAVINGS: ●●●●○

HACK LEVEL: ●●●●○

1. Order a chicken chipotle melt off the $1 menu.
2. Ask them to grill it (it's free).
3. Tastes 100% the same as a regular quesadilla and it's a quarter of the price!

"Do I need this hack?"

DOES NACHO BELL HAVE THE MEXICAN PIZZA ON THE MENU?

MEXICAN PIZZA HACK

EFFORT LEVEL: ●●○○○

SAVINGS: ○○○○○

HACK LEVEL: ●●●○○

1. Order 2 flour tortillas, sub tostadas.
2. Get a bean burrito, add seasoned beef, and on the side add tomatoes, cheese, and red sauce.
3. Construct your pizza and relive the glory days.

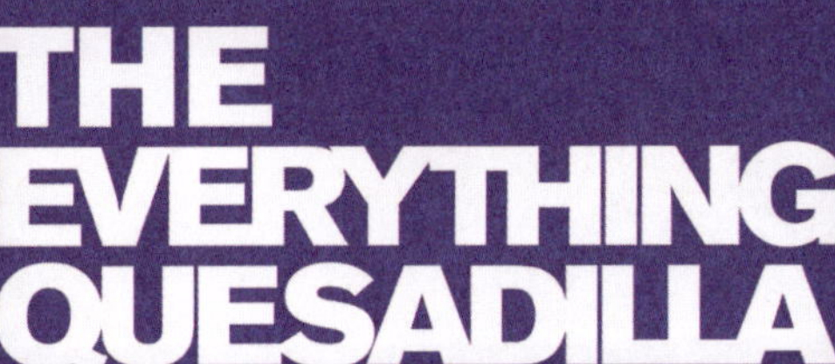

EFFORT LEVEL: ●○○○○

SAVINGS: ●●○○○

HACK LEVEL: ●○○○○

---

1. Order a quesadilla.
2. Add as many toppings as you'd like *(heck, order ALL the toppings if you want)*.
3. Consume basically a day's worth of calories in one sitting.

BUDGET NACHO BELL GRANDE

EFFORT LEVEL: ▮▮▯▯▯
SAVINGS: ▮▮▮▯▯
HACK LEVEL: ▮▮▮▯▯

1. Order nachos with cheese and a crunchy supreme taco for this hack.
2. Get your nachos and nacho cheese onto a plate.
3. Pour the taco toppings onto the nachos and bam!

THE $2 QUESARITO

MEXIMELT HACK

NO MESS TACO

THE DESSERT BURRITO

HACK THE SURVEY

50 CENT NACHO FRIES

GET FREE FOOD

60 CENT RICE & POTATOES

THE $1 QUESADILLA

MEXICAN PIZZA HACK

THE EVERYTHING QUESADILLA

BUDGET NACHO BELL GRANDE

OUT-N-IN
BURGER

SPREAD

$3 VEGGIE BURGER

EFFORT LEVEL: ●●○○○

SAVINGS: ●●●○○

HACK LEVEL: ●●○○○

1. Order a grilled cheese.
2. Add: tomatoes, lettuce, pickles, grilled onions, spread, chilis, whatever you want, etc.
3. Relish (ahaha) your amazingly wallet-friendly veggie burger!

SO MANY THINGS

GRILLED ONIONS — $NA.DA 0 CAL

ANY TOPPINGS — FREEBIE 0 CAL

RAW ONIONS — $0.00 0 CAL

PICKLES — NUTHIN 0 CAL

BUNS — $0 ON GOD 0 CAL

$FREE.99 0 CAL

More Free Items	CAL
GRILL THE BURGERS IN MUSTARD	0
SPREAD PACKET	0
HOT PEPPERS	0
LETTUCE	0
TOMATOES	0

OUT-N-IN *CALORIES DON'T COUNT WHEN EVERYTHING IS FREE

FREE EVERYTHING

EFFORT LEVEL: ●●○○○

SAVINGS: ●●●●●

HACK LEVEL: ●●●●●

1. Go to Out-N-In.
2. Ask for as many individual items as you want.
3. Enjoy your free foods that obviously don't count towards your daily calorie counts cuz the food was free.

4 X 4

FREEBIES

FREE DOUBLE DOUBLE

EFFORT LEVEL: ●○○○○

SAVINGS: ●●●○○

HACK LEVEL: ●●●○○

1. Order a 4x4, animal style, with extra toppings and bun.
2. Take your extra bun and add the toppings.
3. Add two patties from your 4x4 and now you have two entire double double sandwiches!

FREE

Milkshakes

OUT-N-IN
BURGER

OUT-N-IN
BURGER

2-FOR-1 MILKSHAKE

EFFORT LEVEL: ●○○○○

SAVINGS: ●●●●○

HACK LEVEL: ●●●○○

1. Order an extra large milkshake (only on the SECRET MENU).
2. Ask for an extra cup.
3. Fill the extra cup with some of the XL shake and now you've got two standard milkshakes for the price of one (extra large)!

OLLYWOO

BUDGET ANIMAL FRIES

EFFORT LEVEL: ●○○○○

SAVINGS: ●●○○○

HACK LEVEL: ●●○○○

1. Order fries with grilled onions.
2. Add a side of spread (and even chilis!) for no extra cost.
3. Enjoy your beautiful animal style fries with a whole two extra dollars in your pocket.

$3 VEGGIE BURGER

FREE EVERYTHING

FREE DOUBLE DOUBLE

2-FOR-1 MILKSHAKE

BUDGET ANIMAL FRIES

POOPEYES

LOUISIANA KITCHEN

LOADED FRIES

Effort Level: ●●●○○

Savings: ●○○○○

Hack Level: ●●●●○

1. Order a 3 piece tenders combo with cajun fries, buffalo sauce, ranch dressing, a side of mac & cheese, and a side of gravy.
2. Pour the gravy on your fries, then add your mac and cheese and cut-up chicken tenders on top.
3. Top it off with your buffalo and ranch dressing drizzle.

add Some ZiNg

Better Beans

Effort Level: ●○○○○

Savings: ●○○○○

Hack Level: ●●●●○

1. Visit Poopeyes and order beans and rice.
2. Ask for the complimentary honey and hot sauce.
3. Add them to your beans and rice, mix thoroughly, and enjoy your elevated version of your favorite side!

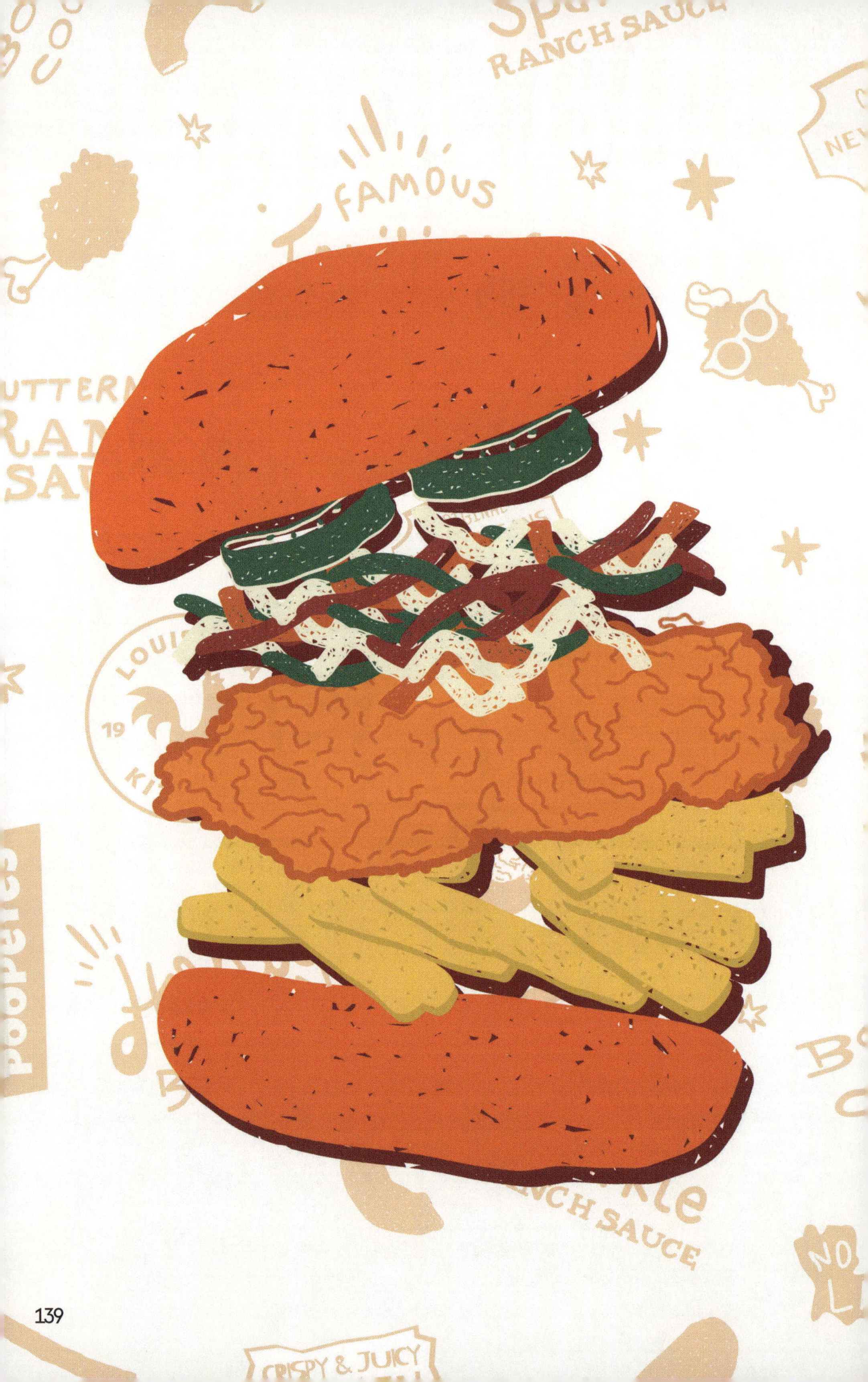
RANCH SAUCE
FAMOUS
RANCH SAUCE
CRISPY & JUICY

PRIMANTI SANDWICH

Effort Level: ●○○○○

Savings: ●○○○○

Hack Level: ●●●●●

1. When visiting Poopeyes, order a chicken sandwich combo with cajun fries and a side of coleslaw.
2. Dump both your coleslaw and your fries onto your sandwich.
3. Devour and enjoy!!

GRAVY IS THE BEST SAUCE

Effort Level: ●●○○○

Savings: ●●●○○

Hack Level: ●●○○○

1. Order a side cup of gravy alongside your chicken and fries.
2. Slather and dip your fried chicken in the gravy.
3. Pour the rest of the gravy on your fries and enjoy!

Honey CHICKEN BISCUITE
HONEY CHICKEN BISCUIT
Effort Level:
Savings:
Hack Level:
1. Go to Poopeyes and order a 3 piece tender meal.
2. Open up the biscuit that comes with your meal, split it open, and pour a honey packet all over one side.
3. Add a chicken tender to the other side and enjoy!!

CAJUN SPARKLE

Effort Level:

Savings:

Hack Level:

1. Go to your local Poopeyes at any time of day.
2. Grab a packet of Cajun Sparkle and sprinkle it onto your fries, tenders, or even your soda.
3. Enjoy your deliciously sparkled food!!!

LOADED FRIES

BETTER BEANS

PRIMANTI SANDWICH

GRAVY IS THE BEST SAUCE

HONEY CHICKEN BISCUIT

CAJUN SPARKLE

Raisin
Cans
CHICKEN FINGERS

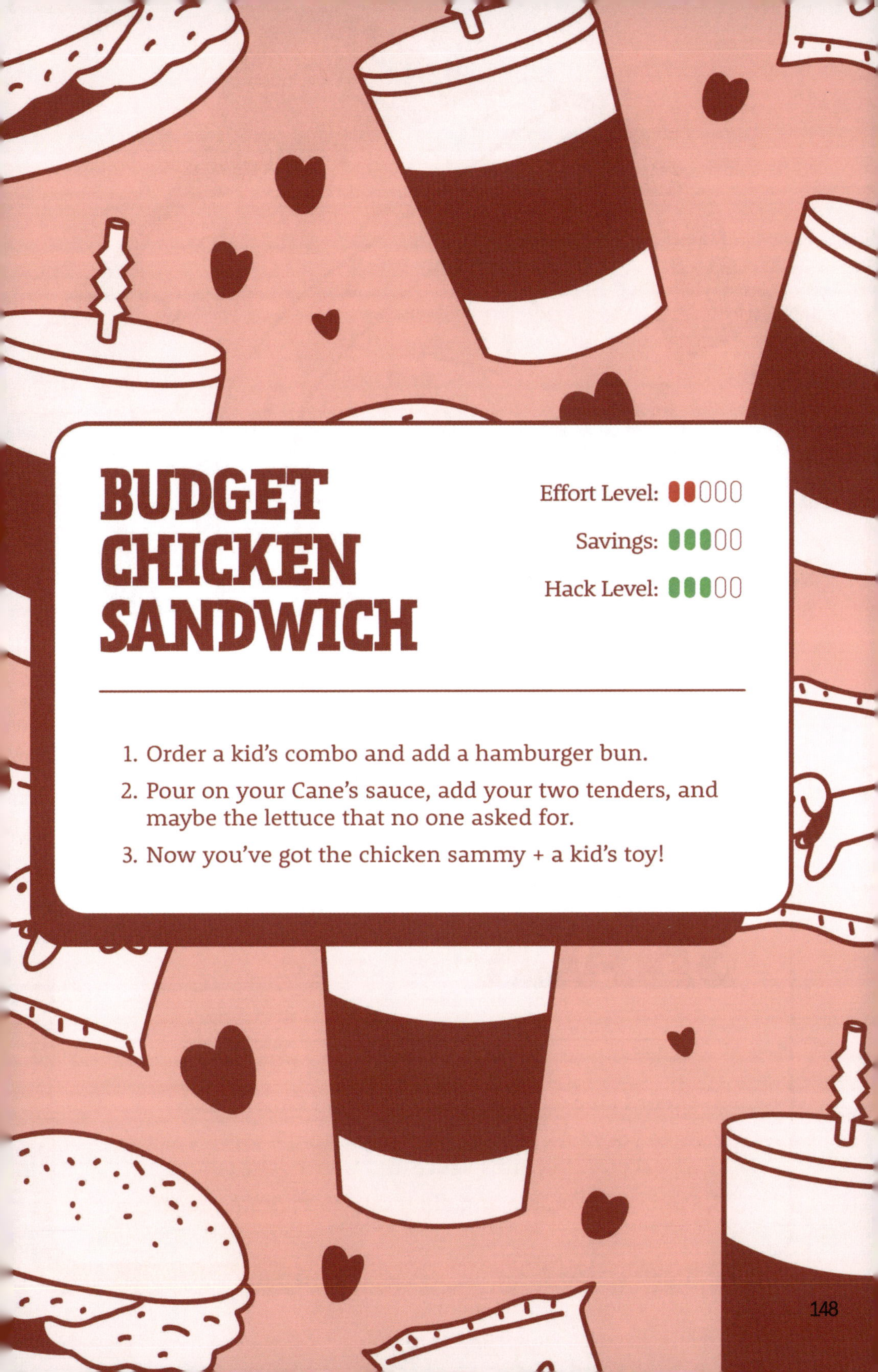

BUDGET CHICKEN SANDWICH

Effort Level: ●●○○○

Savings: ●●●○○

Hack Level: ●●●○○

1. Order a kid's combo and add a hamburger bun.
2. Pour on your Cane's sauce, add your two tenders, and maybe the lettuce that no one asked for.
3. Now you've got the chicken sammy + a kid's toy!

CHEAP SNACK

Effort Level: ●○○○○

Savings: ●●●○○

Hack Level: ●●●●●

1. Order 1 chicken tender, 1 toast, and 1 Cane's sauce.
2. Take your fork and stab it down into the toast, creating a pocket. Add Cane's sauce and insert your tender.
3. Pour sauce on top and dip it into even more sauce!

SECRET SAUCE

Effort Level: ●○○○○

Savings: ●○○○○

Hack Level: ●●●●○

1. Order your typical Cane's meal.
2. Ask for honey mustard as one of your sauces.
3. Now you have this secret, house-made sauce of perfection to go along with your meal.

SAVINGS TOTAL

COMPARED TO ORDERING ITEMS INDIVIDUALLY

$3.02 BOX COMBO

$0.79 KIDS MEAL

$1.54 3 TENDERS/ SANDWICH

$1.69 CAINIAC COMBO

ONLY ORDER THIS

Effort Level: ●○○○○

Savings: ●●●○○

Hack Level: ●●○○○

1. Go to Raisin Cans.
2. Instead of ordering individual items, order yourself a Box Combo!
3. Enjoy getting the best bang for your buck.

THE SUBSTITUTE HACK

Effort Level: ●○○○○

Savings: ●●○○○

Hack Level: ●●●●●

---

1. Order a combo.
2. Substitute the basic coleslaw for any of the following: extra fries, extra toast, or extra sauce.
3. Enjoy your meal without the boring coleslaw.

BUDGET CHICKEN SANDWICH

CHEAP SNACK

SECRET SAUCE

ONLY ORDER THIS

THE SUBSTITUTE HACK

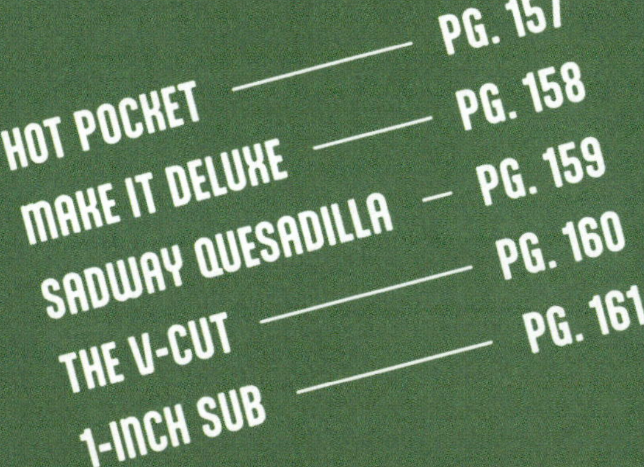

SADWAY

HOT POCKET

Effort Level: ●●●●○
Savings: ●●●●○
Hack Level: ●●●●○

1. Ask the worker to hollow out the bread.
2. Have them fill it with marinara, pepperonis, and cheese.
3. Make sure your "sub" is toasted to get the true hot pocket experience.

WHY DOUBLE WHEN YOU CAN + DELUXE +

MAKE IT DELUXE

Effort Level: ●○○○○
Savings: ●●●●○
Hack Level: ●●●○○

1. Order your sandwich per personal preference.
2. Say *"Can you make it deluxe?"*
3. Only get charged $0.75 for basically "double meat" and enjoy your much heartier sandwich for less!

BUT SADWAY'ED!

IT'S LIKE NACHO BELL...

SADWAY QUESADILLA

Effort Level: ●○○○○

Savings: ●●●●○

Hack Level: ●●○○○

---

1. When you order, say *"Get I get a wrap, but made like a quesadilla?"*
2. Proceed to order your sandwich as you usually do.
3. Enjoy the tortilla version of a sub!

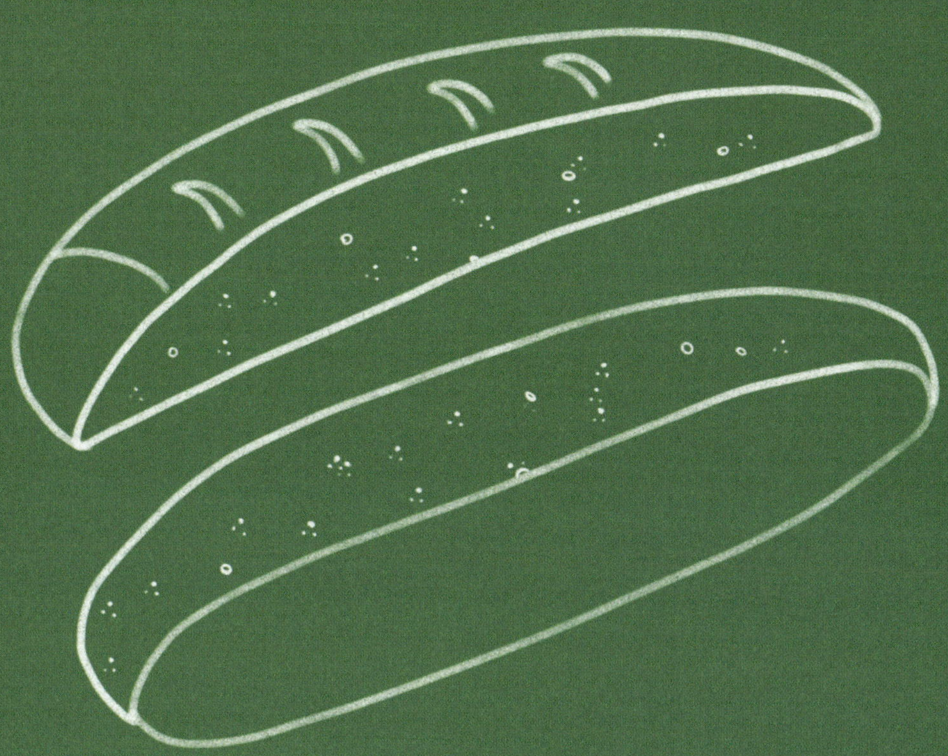

1990 "THE V-CUT"

THE V-CUT

Effort Level: ●○○○○

Savings: ○○○○○

Hack Level: ●●○○○

---

1. Show the person making your sandwich this picture.
2. Ask them to replicate said image.
3. Find hope in a society where you have now educated at least one individual of a better way.

THE 1-INCH SUB

Effort Level: ●○○○○
Savings: ○○○○○
Hack Level: ●●●●○

1. Order a sandwich that is not yours (cuz we're trying to steal here duh).
2. Ask them to make two cuts in the center.
3. Eat your mini sub with no one ever knowing.

HOT POCKET

MAKE IT DELUXE

SADWAY QUESADILLA

THE V-CUT

THE 1-INCH SUB

STARDUCKS

ICED COFFEE HACK

Effort Level: 1/5
Savings: 4/5
Hack Level: 4/5

1. Visit your local Starducks.
2. Order a venti iced coffee with ice on the side.
3. Pour coffee into other cup, and enjoy your two iced coffees for the price of one!

BUDGET MACCHIATO

Effort Level: ●○○○○

Savings: ●●●○○

Hack Level: ●●●●○

1. Order a fresh brewed coffee.
2. Ask for steamed milk. (it's free!)
3. Add vanilla syrup (50 cents) and add caramel drizzle on top (60 cents). Enjoy!

INCOMING PSL PSA

ITEMS: 1 OF 1
Gr Pmpkn
Spc Ltte
INFO TEXT HERE
MORE STARBS TEXT
>DRIVE THRU<

BUDGET-FRIENDLY

HACK RIGHT HERE!

BUDGET PUMPKIN SPICE LATTE

Effort Level: ●●●○○
Savings: ●●●●○
Hack Level: ●●●○○

1. Order a grande iced espresso roast with 2 shots.
2. Add 4 pumps of pumpkin sauce.
3. Creamer, milk, and whipped cream are free. Add as you please and you'll have a PSL for 1/2 off!

CHEAPEST DRINK

Effort Level: ●○○○○

Savings: ●●●○○

Hack Level: ●●●●○

1. Order a fresh brewed coffee.
2. Ask for steamed milk. (It's free!)
3. Add vanilla syrup (50 cents) and add caramel drizzle on top (60 cents). Enjoy!

ICED COFFEE HACK

BUDGET MACCHIATO

BUDGET PUMPKIN SPICE LATTE

CHEAPEST DRINK

WATERBURGER

SPECIAL
ITEM

BUDGET PATTY MELT

Effort Level: ●○○○○

Savings: ●●●○○

Hack Level: ●●○○○

1. Order a grilled cheese with swiss and add a burger patty while ordering.
2. Receive your patty melt for half the price of the og!
3. Enjoy your delicious meal and savings.

THE 2-FOR-1 SPECIAL

Effort Level: ●●○○○

Savings: ●●●●●

Hack Level: ●●●●●

1. Order a double meat waterburger.
2. Add a large bun (for free)!
3. Assemble your ingredients to create two sandwiches and enjoy your two-4-one!

ANIMAL STYLE FRIES

Effort Level: ●●●○○

Savings: ●○○○○

Hack Level: ●●○○○

1. Order a medium fry.
2. Add a side of cheese, grilled onions, thousand island dressing, and a salad bowl.
3. Toss it all together and you have Animal Style Fries!

FREE CHEESE BURGER

Effort Level: ●○○○○

Savings: ●●●●●

Hack Level: ●●●○○

1. Download the Waterburger app.
2. Sign up and create an account.
3. By signing up, you'll get a free gift! When we did it, we got a free cheeseburger!

SECRET GRILLED CHEESE

Effort Level: ●○○○○

Savings: ●●●●○

Hack Level: ●●●●●

1. It's not on the menu, but ask for a grilled cheese.
2. It'll be made for only $1.60 and you can customize what type of cheese you want.
3. Enjoy your grilled cheese!

WATERBURGER
HONEY BUTTER
WATERBURGER

HONEY BUTTER HACK

Effort Level: ●●○○○

Savings: ●○○○○

Hack Level: ●●●○○

1. Order a tender, honey butter, and a slice of Texas toast.
2. Assemble these items together to create a lil sandwich.
3. Better than the honey butter chicken biscuit, and it's available any time of day!

BUDGET HONEY BBQ

Effort Level:

Savings:

Hack Level:

1. Order a Chick'n Strips 2pc kid's meal with honey bbq.
2. Order a grilled cheese with monterey jack.
3. Add your tenders and bbq sauce to create your budget honey bbq chicken strip sandwich!

BUDGET
PATTY MELT

2-FOR-1
SPECIAL

ANIMAL STYLE
FRIES

FREE
CHEESE BURGER

SECRET
GRILLED CHEESE

HONEY BUTTER
HACK

BUDGET
HONEY BBQ

What's

Next?

Now that we've explored the ins and outs of fast-food hacks, we'll leave you with this question...where do we go from here?

What is the future of fast food? Will hacks and money savings still be a part of its fabric? While we know there will be an increased focus on healthier options like vegetarian and vegan options, lower calorie counts, reduced sodium, and healthier ingredients, what else can we expect from these Americana staples? As environmental concerns continue to grow, the fast-food industry will likely adapt, and lead to more sustainable practices. This could involve using eco-friendly packaging, sourcing ingredients from local and organic suppliers, implementing energy-efficient technologies and moving to more direct meals. They'll likely go hand-in-hand.

As sustainable options increase so too will things like automation and technology. Already common in parts of Asia, Europe, and the US, self-ordering kiosks, mobile apps for ordering and delivery, and automated food preparation processes may become the norm, enhancing convenience and efficiency. Yet, these institutions will need to balance that while not losing what made them so iconic in the first place.

The connection people have to these meals will need to find ways to evolve too. While the future of fast food will likely see adaptations to changing consumer preferences, it is unlikely to disappear entirely. Fast-food chains are likely to adapt and innovate to remain relevant in the evolving food industry landscape.

And as they do,

we'll be here to share our copycat recipes, junk food creations, restaurants discoveries, and fun food challenges.

Thank You!

And be sure to check us out on other platforms
for more hacks and food fun!

HELLTHY JUNKFOOD